Andalucía
Lisa Marie Basile

Published by Brothel Books
Copyright © 2011 by Lisa Marie Basile

ISBN-13: 978-0983421719
ISBN-10: 0983421714
First Printing, October 2011

Cover Art: Ernie Sandige
Cover Design: Alyssa Morhardt-Goldstein

Brothel Books
The Poetry Society of New York
New York, New York
brothelbooks.com

Love for The Poetry Society of New York and to the talented poets within The Poetry Brothel. Thank you, Ernie Sandige for your incredible cover art. Stephanie Berger, thank you for supporting this manuscript in all its forms and coming with me to the Andalucía we see here. Mama, Lee, I can hear you inside sea-shells.

Sincere thanks and acknowledgements to *PANK* Magazine for publishing versions of four of the poems within this collection (pages two, three, four & five).

Leñador.
Córtame la sombra.
Líbrame del suplicio
de verme sin toronjas.

Woodcutter.
Cut my shadow from me.
Free me from the torment
of seeing myself without fruit.

— Federico García Lorca

Andalucía

I ate my own body
in parlors of no color,
to the bone, to the hooves. I become
so thin I buckle under myself. I am
a mane of white on fire.

Andalucía wears masks
of red, death red. I have become obsessed:
decadence: dark wine: damp skin.

I am obsessed with your outreached hands,
your continental shutters parted and your hourglass
eternally tumbling with the tides.

Andalucía, I am thin for you.
        How I am engulfed by you.

When I see Alejandro I do not wear shoes. Because
the sand is soft and the soft is always expanding and
he likes to look at me! *me* flickering through all of his
rooms, watering his garden, wearing aprons and
reading books I do not understand.

I cannot trust myself with books. Books with words:
Even Eden was tainted.

> No one means to carry their burdens
> to good places.

If I wear shoes it will compel me to leave so I stay
down like a sea without nerve or hunger and I speak
in tongues things of obedience, things of sex in the
morning while Spain watches and sometimes I think
she judges me, Spain, she is a woman who knows
about being conquered and conquering and
Alejandro says I am partial to my madness, that I
ought to make him lemon water and make him love.
We condemn our palaces, I say.

I am drugged by moon shine and sea-salt.
Your eyes are bloodshot, he says. *Sleep.*
Before I sleep, I ask, *where am I?*

Andalucía.
Bad girls go to Andalucía.

How do I explain Andalucía?
I went there and saw myself
unfolding. I did not miss anything
from my first life, and this scared me.

How do I explain Andalucía?
The necromancy of bones on bones.
One white mare upon a ship,
sailing the horse latitudes,
the tango of daytime owls. Bleeding

into new forms, watching your life, a disease,
through a powerful lens, watching
through the holes of a blood doily
  to see the failed city under the sea.

A dead mother draped over the child
she could not save, a shawl of skin and love.
An impossibly slow flamenco.
Slower still: a nightmare where you are
always overdressed and cannot move.

Why don't I want to leave?
I can barely speak the language.

Andalucía, we are in an abusive relationship.

Alejandro stalked me when I ran away — from
Gibraltar to Barcelona — and he saw me from the
street and said: *bona tarda!* like some kind of devil.

His hair slicked back & shiny leather shoes. Black
and white flowers fell from his mouth. I potted them
inside me. I could not run away!

Late in the night we had more cava, dined
under the castle Montjuic. The castle fed me thoughts
of death.

How could I leave a place with castles?
How could I leave a world of youth and balconies?
How could I abandon pure beauty and thin legs and
dark holes? Why do we resurrect the love
and pain we knew as children?

Alejandro sings in Catalan, I saw my father in his
song. I saw my father in his face. I started to mouth
the words *you look so much like my father* when the
castle said *no baby, don't bring your pain to dinner.*

All the Alejandros in the garden!

There are tears for miles, and inky cherubs
everywhere. My addictions to the ocean
and to lies.

Alejandro looks at me. He is just a marionette,
a man given orders, a snakelike priest,
a sea-speaker.

The Alejandros heave and sound the drum-roll of
ancient civilizations. Somewhere

inside me he clobbers a beast and I tend to a child.
Somewhere

inside me I clobber a beast and he is a child,
and there was my childhood, my knobby knees,
              the need to be beautiful.

And there laid the collateral
of me, weaknesses
that smelled like the Mediterranean.

You don't need a sea to be happy

                    do you?

Mother sits covered in veils, facing the wall of
Montjuic, fuzzy worms and blood oranges up the
walls, Manet painting bridges from me to her and
from me again, and when I cross to lift the veil, the
colors collapse. Mother disappears.

Reach out, she says, *my bouganvilla.* But I can't
reach, not through the salty smelling dolor. Not
toward her, already gone   she is
disappointed in me.

Do you remember when you had my hips?
The hips of the sea, wide eternal, mysterious.
New and unknown lives live inside your hips.

(Do I remember when I loved myself more than
castles? How my hips are castles!)

My mother is a satchel of insects flitting away from
me. She wants to find the light. Her monarchs fly
Eastward. Their atomic shadows against the apron of
some sun, the last quantum bit of her wing song.

Is it more painful to mourn for your mother or watch
your mother mourn for you?

She says, *all you need to exist is contentment. How
can you disappear if you're not sure you've existed?
Have you ever even been here, baby?*

I am midnight in Barcelona. You can hear the fold of
lip on teeth:

Mitjanit

Here I have found the time inside caverns
        of drunken butterflies.

Do I look like *that* when I drink? Do I flutter
stupidly against countries and men and lovers?
Dusting off my own ability to fly in return
for some petty petting? Hell is other people.

In nightmares
when I was living, I could never
read or interpret the time on clocks.

In Andalucía it is always 33 o'clock,
the time when ships sail the 33rd parallel,
the time when sailors throw horses
off the sides of ships, voyages too long,
too long, too long,

and I gallop through all seas,
day and night, seeking. Seeking.

I don't know
what I am
seeking.

Mother says *approval.* For all eternity,
she'll say *approval.* Until you know that wanting
beauty is purgatory, until you stop wanderlusting
continents
and bodies
of water.

Time walks up walls on stilts
and falls again,
and here I am Sisyphus
possessed by flamenco.
I am always dancing or flying or running.
I just want to be looked at, tamed, groomed.
      I want to run
the outline of Spain
faster than the other beasts,
      want to taste
the fullness of the sea's tempranillo,
      want to make Alejandro see me.

Did you wake up in Andalucía? Did you make fools of your hooves? Are you always on fire?
Do you repeat yourself again and again and again and again? Did you fall into the sea? Are you ever in pain? Are you always in pain? Did you ever appreciate your eyesight? Did you keep looking into mirrors? Do you like what you see? Did you ever feel comfortable alone? Did you ever hold your hands like a lover? Did you binge on your own human heart? Did you scoop out your eyes so you wouldn't look? Did you drop a dead horse off the side of your ship? Did you ever kill a sailor? Did you walk away empty? Did you let them love you? Do you eat too much red meat? Did you run toward the decadent to hide in its shadow? Are you always on fire? Did you drink black wine to keep your mouth full & shut? Did you sleep, ever, without needing anything but sleep? Did you walk away from the castles? Did you ever hide your skin under the table? Did you eat to conquer? Did you comfort a stranger today? Do you need to be comforted? Are you always on fire? Do you smoke too many cigarettes? Did you sail for too long seeking? Did you find the approval you need? Did you inherit a sickness? Did you blame god? Do you believe in God? Do you believe in yourself? Are you still on fire? Did you ever put out the fire? Did you ever let god mold you? Did you let man mold you? Did you ever mold yourself in an image of god? Do you believe in the image of God? Do you believe in your own image? Did you ever say no? Did you ever say no? Did you ever say no I won't? Did you say no when you wanted to say no? Did you keep your shoes off so you wouldn't leave? Did you drink the sea until you were thirsty?

Dreams. In them, Alejandro
says *when you want too much
you end up in Andalucía.*

He speaks backwards, speaks in neighs,
gallopthroated, but I like a talkative, handsome
centaur. We can ride together.

Dreams. In them, there is Dolores,
who hides nothing. She cleans the floor on her knees,
cries into soap.

Tears all over her speckled leopard skin.
She bellows; her sorrow is pornographic.
All of us are animals. I feel my obsessions morphing
into wings, so heavy so repetitive I can't stop flying.
My heart becomes a horse in a stall.

Dreams. In them, I meet Alejandro and he tells me
he's planted a field. He wants everyone to look at his
colors.

When I look, there is nothing but dried leaves.
I dig with a thousand naked blades but, no!
No color   no life   underneath.   Nothing
but Atlantis.

The good garden, the good civilization
once Utopian, failed by mirrors and skin.
I mourn. My hands pulling up the ocean, piling waves
to the side. How do I get home? I mourn.

Alejandro says everyone mourns. Even centaurs
mourn. Even mourning, even night.

Here, the teacups have scales.
When I put one down, it walks away!
When I look in the mirror
it is me all wrapped up in a bloody bonnet,
me morphed and broken, my face holding
my face in its hands, recognizing I must have
put myself here, dwelling on the sicknesses
of self and skin. And when I place the porcelain
for my dinner party, all the little saucers shatter.
I pour from myself the wine of my heart,
and no one drinks. These tapas are worms,
are blood, are weaving through the lace of the table
and up the legs of old chairs. Rain falls,
and I am suddenly aware of myself or the déjà vu of
myself and that part of me is somewhere
else, maybe just my elbows even.
Perhaps my scapula? My bones?
Perhaps a belief
in god or myself?

I spent my sleep with Dolores again, with her fat little
legs grinding into the clay. She shapes pots and vases
under the sun. She gives these gifts to the blind.
These are tear-jars. A whole factory of tears and clay.

> The pang of constant need.
> I wonder why she is living
> in Andalucía.
> How can an old woman suffer so?

There are operas inside of her jars.
Her years, her heart's hooves running
from the mourning.

My ears sink and swim inside, I hear a whole world
watching itself build and burn and burn and build
catacombs.

Dolores says,
*I am attracted to all kinds of love
like a moth without a path. I am attracted to centaurs
who trample me. I am attracted to atomic light.
I keep galloping on fire.*

I can hear it repeating in the shells,
in the tear jars.

Dreams.
In them mother says I can go home
                    if I can find the way.

Dolores. She tells me about nests of prowling
animals, troubled seas. Dark wine. Fat old bodies
and golden men, a continental carousel
spinning you on hounds and leopards. She says, you
see yourself in your youth standing in white sand.
You see your health. You see your blood for the first
time. You see someone walking away in the mist. You
are the mist. You see your eyes red and swollen. You
see your sickness getting under satin covers. Your
eyes become so painful you're forbidden to cry. You
start to wake up, still travelling, still holding that
pearly column, still circles, eyes on fire, circling, still
watching the rotation of the tigers and the music, and
of the earth itself, still smelling sea-salt, still tilting and
falling, still wanting perfection, still on fire, still
needing a man who will be easy and say stay, stay. Still
staying down like crouching horses in a white field,
obedient, still in stalls. Still struck by decadence and
lace-covered hooves, still speaking in tongues, still
seeing the number 33 everywhere, still chasing
freedom inside sea-shells, golden men and new
languages. The abuse: the globe luring you with
pointy fingers: you running off to the sea. You
running off to find yourself in the sea. You wanting to
be prettier than the sea, you wanting to become the
sea. You looking at your reflection in the water,
seeing Dolores, old and eternal. Miserable Dolores.

There are certain
places in Andalucía:

>   kelp becomes body armor
>   thunder learns to speak Spanish
>   sirens sing for themselves

Somewhere across the Mediterranean
a small pale girl listens into a shell and understands.

>   There are places in Andalucía
>   doorways out,
>   where you can grow teeth again,

where you bite yourself
out of cocoons. You can bite
yourself out of cocoons.

You don't need
anyone else's teeth.

I wear short dresses when I visit Alejandro. *You have legs for many miles,* he says. So I show them. If I take my legs away, would he still see me? I come to water his flowers, to comb his hair, to linger on his skin. I am the mosquito, but he drinks my blood. He sleeps on the floor, on his back. He is covered in flies. I step over Alejandro, and his fingers linger on my toes. He is wet from seas. I step again over him, teasing, teasing. I cannot seem to feed all the flowers. The red ones, the hard ones. The fat ones. They grow. I cannot tame them. I cannot groom them. I cannot control them. I say hola and they grow and grow. The more we talk the more they grow, and we talk, and we talk. We talk about beauty and the way a body is supposed to look. We talk about the way a woman should be shaped and we talk about my hips, my lips. Too round, too powerful, too godlike. *You cannot trust a woman who looks like a woman,* he says. *She might destroy you.* Look, I am unribboning! My bones are peeling as petals. I am hungry. I say I cannot seem to stop stepping over and over him. *You know that I look up your dress every time,* he tells me. I know that. I know that is how I can keep him there, buzzing. I am burlesque vultures swooping overhead, and it feels good. Dolores shakes her head.

Dolores says
>
> *when you lose sight of yourself*
> *you wake up in Andalucía,*
> the very gateway toward
> here   and there.

Alejandro's lullaby,
sand grouses chirping
        outside the window
hundreds of mares
galloping through a burning field. Neighing,
coming apart. They were pure and good once, and
now they're just animals
running off into watery cliffs.

Fear, that old equalizer
Mama said.

A quiet humming
across the ocean's surface,
its salty hands trying to reach the red,
to cool the burn.

Sometimes
I am the water,

                and sometimes
                I am the fire.

Sometimes you remember dying in the sea
but who can be so sure?

Let us smoke and dance and drink,
Alejandro says. We are in the ring, I am a drunken
bull and he is my matador. I charge.

We jitterbug the ring, me all satin mane,
he all traje de negro. We are carousels
spinning out. I can see glimpses of my real
self on every turn, asking me to abandon the animals,
abandon my horns.

Our heal and toe, our pirouette,
         whipping the hip, left to right,
we are red-lipped and long-gloved,

with old dead dogs
and old women barking
at us. They are betting on me,
they want me to tear the cape,
to grown horns. I taste
gore in my mouth and love it.

I eat Alejandro
                    Alive.

Here cadavers regulate my movements.
I am relearning how to move with these new parts,
these new arms, these arms always reaching out
and never in.

Here I am a mummy, never really dead. Am forever
designed to want and want and never be full. Here I
am in the Iberian Peninsula, stuck between the
second and third gates, always desiring, never full,
never seeing myself in mirrors.

My arms up around Alejandro's face, and I can
barely stand. There are ghosts on porches staring.
Ghosts are daggers. And, my mother with the veil
over her head. She is sitting idly in a chair, adorned
with lemons and slowly mouthing
you have
> *done something*
>> *terribly wrong!*

I feel his wet on my neck, like a hungry infant.
> Spitting up.

My mother shakes her head, remembers when I was
an infant, was a decent infant, spitting up.

All of Andalucía dances. Like elefantes trampling tiny
things. Like dragons. We are frightened of ourselves.
We are the fugitives of sorrow. We dance in circles
and sometimes gnash our teeth. Our legs are so fused
to the dance that we become boney mares running,
running off of the continental walls and into the sea.
If we spin quickly enough, we see ourselves in the
periphery, ourselves so kind and our skin so full, and
our desires clean, cool sand. Ourselves so
human. Forgiving of ourselves. Forgiving of our
humanity, of our desire to be godlike.

Today I almost saw my mother. These things happen in a flash, these things happen sometimes. Sometimes it's from drinking too much cava, or too much ocean. I was galloping, Alejandro behind me. His hooves in my footsteps, my hooves in his. He was a sun centaur, still half man, still convincing. I wanted my body back, my breasts. I wanted my skin back. I wanted to wear my anatomy as a necklace. I wanted to stop the fire, to save my hair. I once had the hair of sirens, my fibula, my ligaments, my humanity, my capillaries, my mighty spine. And then, I saw myself holding baskets of small fish, flopping. I threw them back into the sea. My hands were wet and hopeful. I stood in the shape of a chapel. Alejandro was not there, and I almost wasn't guilty and I almost was free. I was almost sudden birds migrating. I almost migrated on two legs, two human legs.

You might be rid of transgressions
               but o, they're not rid of you.

I ate the body. I tackled it against the ring.
I ate seas and grew a crown of salt and flies.
I planted babies in flower pots,
and I watched blue fingers grow.

I drowned good things in cava.
Soon   a new baby grew up
and looked like me,
half leaves. Black-toothed. Soil tongue.

The things we pass on
we pass on silently. Plant the dead,
and who knows what might grow.
Bury the dead and you might go

with them. You might try to resuscitate
yourself by forking continents and men
and dark meat into your mouth,
mouthfuls, and mouthfuls. You give

yourself up to purgatory. You find
the gate and walk through.
Here the flowers do not eat light.
Here you miss the soft and simple you,

the you that you were before.

What if it feels good to me, walking through eternal
firey stalls? What if I'm happy to be a sinner, to drink
red until my skin turns.

To glimpse my former life — the happiness,
the calm quiet of an afternoon, so what?
To etch the entire Iberian Peninsula into my skin,

the bouganvillas, the little bloody tapas:
finger tips and femurs and cracked mirrors. To live
on the seaside with gluttony and lust as lovers.

To wear myself like a cloak with a human head and
jaguar spine. To sail forever never finding land.
What if I am strong enough

        to live with the presque vu?
        The almost cupping
        of my former life in my hands.
        The resignation.

I fill pots with tears
for miles stretching
only to look inside
and find them empty again.

I wake up, or so it seems, to Dolores carving lemons
out, mixing them into a pitcher of water. She drops
the seeds into a pile.
Dozens of seeds, piling.

   How much lemon water are you making?
She turns to me, with her face of fragments.
She is the closed eyes of Odilon Redon.
   I do not know.

Why does everyone believe the dead are suddenly
so patient?

I count six thousand lemons in the wet and colorless
ground. They are corneas
watching,
watching me
me taking knives from her
her carving lemons forever
forever so long   so long
I forget how to speak,
     and o, I like to speak!

We stare out at the marketplace, the sand.
There are souls for sale chained to cornstalks.
We could use a few for the garden.
We could be friends.

I am with my mother again in the sea!

She is as beautiful as ever, the same rouge lips, torn-off kitchen apron. Those rebellious green eyes.

The water has pulled in and is waiting, chained back by some devils, waiting to curl back from its paralysis. She is sitting on the edge of an old chaise longue, and there are exoskeletons clinging to the curled feet. The time, it is almost dusk, and when she points to me, she says

*When you will you accept
that you have become Atlantis?*

The white sand becomes very, very black. Only starfish can be seen, framing the remnant of my mother's sallow face as the offing swoops in as a thousand liquid sparrows.

*(It always felt so good to see my mother exasperated,
but this is different.
This is eternal.)*

It all felt very normal.

There were Dixieland echoes bleeding up the edges
of trees, and I wanted to be beautiful, and I wanted to
be horses and egrets and vultures and bulls and
jaguars. How I had lost my femininity in the fist of the
sea. How we leave ourselves as forgotten cities, our
hearts later hypothesized and missed. I wanted to be
on fire forever. I wanted to drink tear jars. I wanted to
be loved by everyone.

There were hornets circling around a tiny child
covered in honey at the base of a tree. I wanted to
destroy the sun. I wanted to hide inside castles. And
the child, Alejandro's child, was me, and she held a
tiny milky dagger toward the sky and with her fat pink
face, my pink face, we were accepted into Andalucía.
I could not remember my mother's name.

I could not remember my name. I was a baby, his
baby — teething on the continental shelf. Reborn, or
never dead, I caught a flash of the old me, the good,
kind me. Flashes, flashes. Flashes every 33 feet under
water, the old me down there,
the pressure, the bends my funeral gown.

They ate the baby
until her eyes
                    my eyes
were as vacant as the sea.

Lisa Marie Basile lives in Brooklyn. She is the author of *A Decent Voodoo* (Cervena Barva Press, 2012), *Triste* (Dancing Girl Press, 2012) and a collaborative chapbook, *Diorama* (Wisp Press, 2011). She has recently been published in *PANK, kill author, elimae, The Scrambler, Pear Noir!, Moon Milk Review* and others.

An M.F.A. in writing candidate at The New School, Lisa Marie also performs for The Poetry Brothel as Luna Liprari. She is the founding editor of <u>Patasola Press</u> and reads poetry for <u>*Weave*</u> Magazine. *lisamariebasile.com*

Brothel Books, The Poetry Society of New York's newest imprint, is a small book publisher based in New York City. The Poetry Brothel has long been a proponent of bringing poetry to the masses-- exclusively, and with absolute discretion. Likewise, The Poetry Brothel's publishing arm, Brothel Books, publishes the most intimate, most charming, and most crafted works being produced today, primarily by The Poetry Brothel's poets across the globe, but also the general public. *brothelbooks.com*

Made in the USA
Middletown, DE
05 September 2019